Letts

KEY STAGE 1

Year 2 Term 2

Teaching and Learning

Science

Activity Book

Andrew Hodges
Alan Jarvis
Heather Monaghan

First published 2001

Letts Educational Ltd, The Chiswick Centre,
414 Chiswick High Road, London W4 5TF
Tel: 020 8996 3333
Fax: 020 8742 8390
www.letts-education.com

Series editor: Alan Jarvis
Designed, edited and produced by Gecko Limited, Cambridge
Cover design: Santamaria
Illustrations: Mike Atkinson, Rachel Conner, Peter Geissler

British Library Cataloguing-in-Publication Data
A CIP record for this book is available from the British Library

ISBN 1 84085 547 9

Printed in the UK

Letts Educational Ltd, a division of Granada Learning Ltd.
Part of the Granada Media Group.

Contents

How to use this book

In this book you will learn about the food and exercise you need to stay healthy. You will also find out how different plants and animals live and grow in different places. Plants and animals are alike in some ways and different in others. You will learn how we use this to sort them into groups.

Look out for these.

Emma can kick and gurgle.

Captions tell you about the picture.

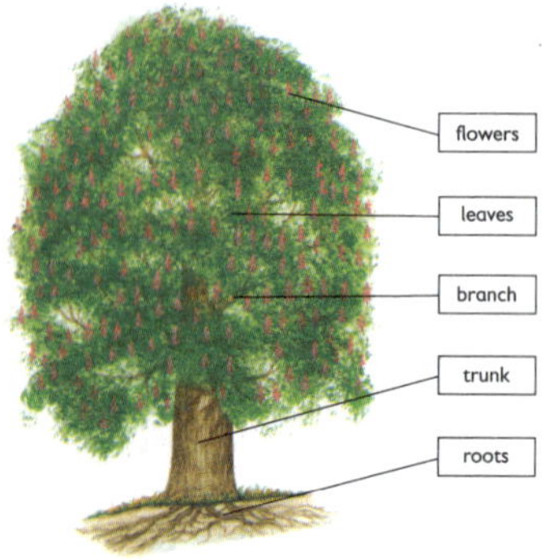

Labels tell you the names of parts of the picture.

Speech bubbles tell you what the children are saying.

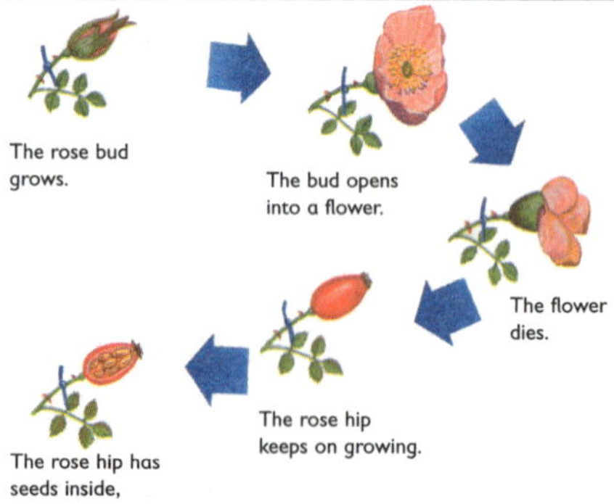

Arrows tell you what to look at next.

Health and growth

You will learn:
- that you need a variety of foods to grow well.
- how to group foods.
- that you need exercise to keep healthy.
- that animals produce young.
- about the differences between babies and toddlers.
- that you need to take care when you use medicines.
- how to collect data and fill in charts.

Plants and animals in the local environment

You will learn:
- that different plants and animals live in different places.
- that flowering plants produce seeds which grow into new plants.
- that animals reproduce and change as they get older.
- how to plan tests to find out about plants.
- how to make tests fair.

Variation

You will learn:
- about the differences between animals and plants.
- that all animals are alike in some ways and different in others.
- that humans are alike in some ways and different in others.
- that plants are alike in some ways and different in others.
- about the parts of plants.
- how to measure some differences between humans.
- that you can sort animals into different groups.

Humans need food and water to stay alive. You need a variety of foods to grow

Clare ate these meals yesterday.

Breakfast

Lunch

Evening meal

What do you like to eat for your meals?
Draw what you ate for each meal yesterday.
Label your drawing.

Clare sometimes eats snacks and has drinks between meals.

Snacks

Drinks

What drinks do you like? Draw a drink for each of the meals you have drawn.

drink food human

You eat lots of different foods. You can sort these into groups.

Foods in the same group may look and taste different.

These are all fruit.

These are all cereals.

Collect some empty food packets.
Sort them into different groups.

These are all meat.

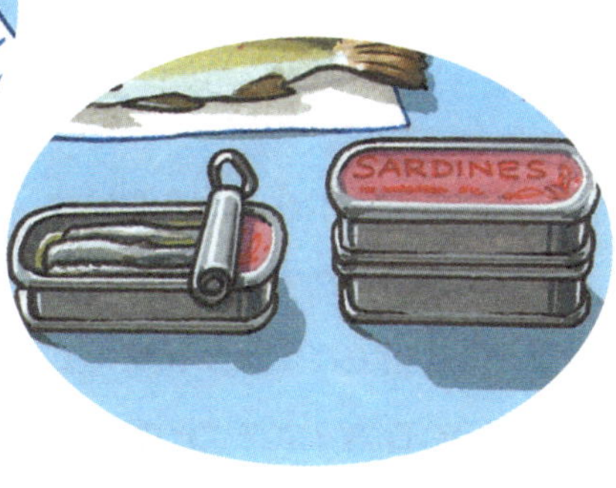

These are all fish.

Think of some more foods that fit in each of these groups.
What is your favourite food? What does it taste like?

food

Favourite foods

We all eat different foods. Everyone has a favourite food.

Mrs Spark's class did a survey. They made a tally chart and a block graph.

Our favourite foods

chocolate	𝍸 III
chips	𝍸 I
oranges	III
beefburgers	𝍸 II
ice cream	𝍸

Our favourite foods

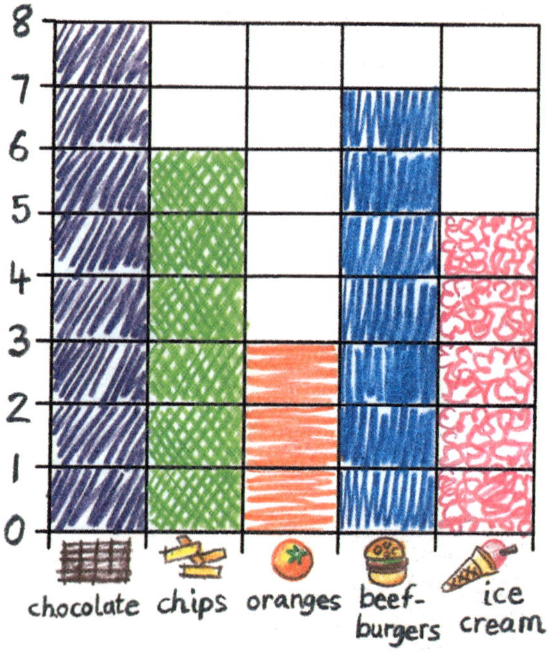

They found out that:
7 children like beefburgers best.
5 children like ice creams best.
3 people like oranges best.
Most children like chocolate best.
More children like chips than ice cream.

**Find out about favourite foods in your class.
You could use the computer to help you.
Write sentences about what you found out.**

Favourite foods

People like to eat some foods on special days. These foods are sometimes different from what they usually eat. These are often treats.

Birthday

Pancake day

Divali

Christmas

Choose a special occasion. Draw and label all the food you would eat for a special meal.

Christmas Divali food tally

We need exercise to keep us fit and healthy. After exercise we often feel hot and tired.

Do you get lots of exercise? Make a list of the things you do at school and home that give you exercise.

Matt and Tim are playing football. They have been running a lot.

How do Matt and Tim feel? How will they feel after they have had a rest?

All animals have young that grow into adults. Some young animals do not look like their parents.

The horse and her foal stay close together.

The swan protects her cygnets.

There are frogs and tadpoles in the pond.

Butterflies lay eggs on leaves. Their caterpillars eat the leaves.

Find the young animals. Which look like their parents? Which are different?

Some animals feed their young and look after them until they are grown up.

The cow gives milk to her calf.

Birds feed their fledglings.

Ducklings swim near to their mother to be safe.

Young rabbits play near their burrow.

Talk about how animals look after their young.

adult parent

Human babies need to be looked after while they grow up.

This is Emma. She is two months old. She is a baby.

Her mother feeds her often . . .

. . . and dresses her.

She changes her nappy.

Do you know a young baby? Who looks after them? What do they have to do?

Emma can kick and gurgle.

Her mother baths her.

Emma sleeps a lot in her pram.

Emma will soon be a toddler. What will she be able to do then?

adult baby human toddler

Sometimes people take medicines when they are ill. It can be dangerous to take medicines at other times.

Ramesh has asthma.

Viv has a cold.

Gordon has burned his arm.

Viv's granny has a weak heart.

Do you know anyone who takes medicine? Talk about the medicine. What is it for?

Some medicines look like sweets. It is important to know what is a sweet and what is a medicine so that we do not eat pills by mistake. They might make us ill.

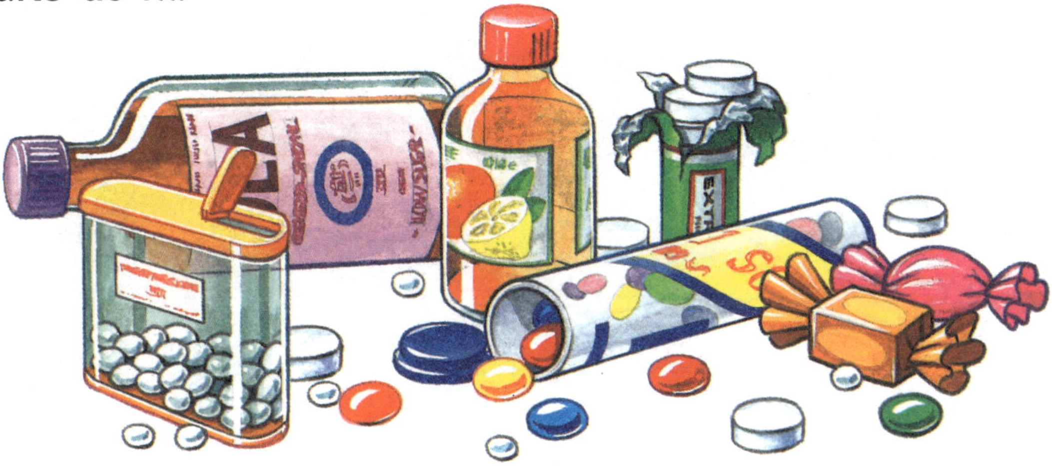

These are sweets and drinks.

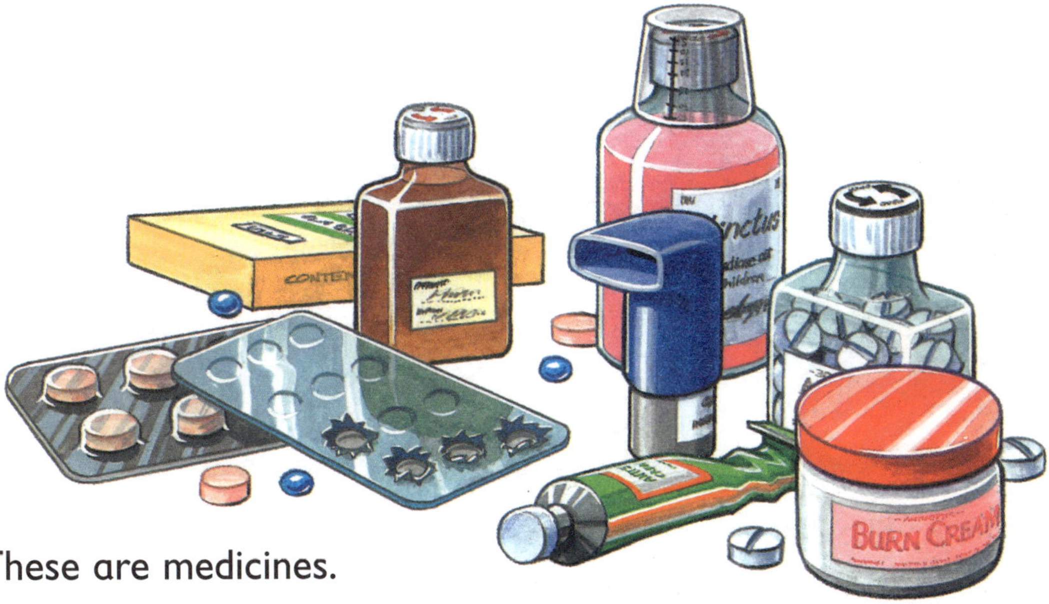

These are medicines.

Medicines should be kept in a safe place so that young children cannot reach them. Draw somewhere to keep medicines. Why is it a good place?

medicine pills

Animals live in a place because of what it is like there.

These animals like dark, damp places among logs and stones.

These animals like open spaces where they can see danger coming. They need bushes nearby where they can hide.

Choose one group of animals. Draw a place where they might live and say what it is like there.

Plants grow in different places too. They all need light and water and most need soil.

These plants can grow roots through cracks between bricks and stones. This means they can grow where there is not much soil.

These plants grow tall among the bushes where the grass is not cut.

Where do animals and plants live around your school? Think of one place. What would you expect to find there?

You can find different kinds of animals and plants where you live.

Mrs Spark's class looked for animals and plants in their school garden.

Sally's group found small animals in the woodpile. They made a tally chart.

Small animals in the wood pile

Look around your school playground.
Find out which animals live there and where they live.
Make a chart to show what you found.

Weeds growing between stones

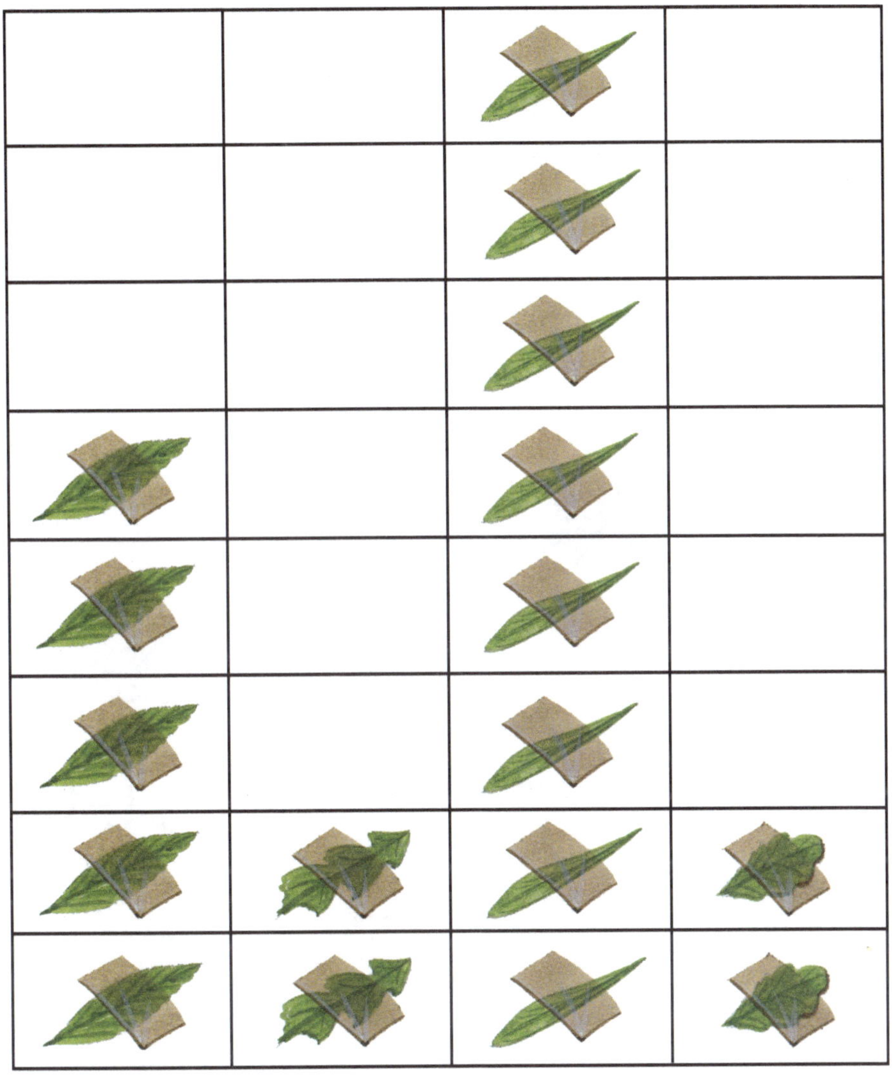

Jamila's group found weeds growing between the stones. They took a leaf from each one and stuck it down to make a pictogram.

What plants can you find growing on the path or among the grass? Make a pictogram.

pictogram **tally**

New plants can grow from seeds. Most plants have flowers. When the flowers die, the fruit grows from part of the flower. The seeds are in the fruit.

This is what happens to one rose bud on a rose bush.

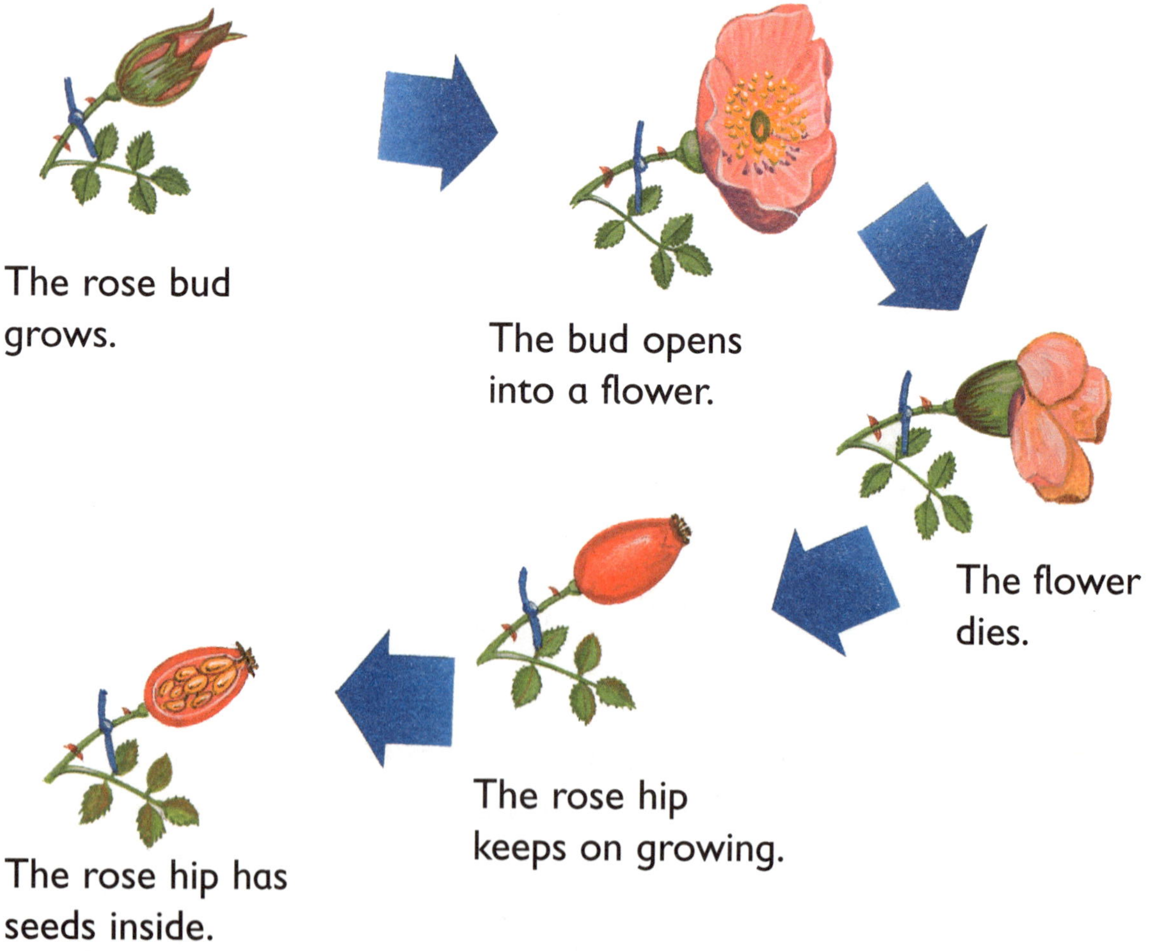

Look at a plant that has dead flowers. Can you see where the seeds are growing?

All these are fruits. They have seeds inside them.

tomato

grapes

avocado

mango

poppy

honesty

Look for plants around your school.
Can you find more seeds?
Take care because some plants and seeds are poisonous.

flower fruit seed

We can talk about where plants grow and where they don't grow. We can test our ideas.

Mrs Spark's class thought of reasons why plants may not grow in some places.

This is Sally's group.

What we think will happen

In soil – will grow a lot
In sand – will grow a bit
On a stone – won't grow

Talk about what they think will happen. Do you think they are right or wrong? It does not matter if they are wrong. They will find out the answer when they do their test.

Will they grow? Plan a test

This is Ed's group.

What we think will happen
Outside – will grow tall
Windowsill – will start to grow
Box – won't grow at all

Have they planned good tests? What do you think will happen? What have you noticed about plants and what they need to grow? Plan your own test.

When we do a test we need to make it fair.

Tim's group tested whether beans need soil to grow. They put the beans in clear plastic pots.

What they did – they changed the kind of soil.

This bean is in soil. This bean is in sand. This bean is on stones.

What they kept the same – they gave them all light and water.

They put all the pots on the windowsill.

They watered all the pots.

Plan a different test for your group. What things will you keep the same so your test is fair?

They looked at the beans every day and drew what happened.

What happened after a week

Bean in soil has a root.

Bean in sand has a root.

Bean on stones has cracked.

What happened after two weeks

Bean in soil has a shoot.

Bean in sand has a shoot.

Bean on stones has a little root.

What they found out – beans don't need soil to start to grow.

They are going to look after their beans until the end of term. Do you think all the beans will grow well?

fair test

Animals can have young which grow into adults.

Birds lay eggs with a shell on. The bird makes a nest and keeps the eggs warm so the chick will grow inside and hatch.

They grow bigger. When she is 18 weeks old, the young hen begins to lay eggs.

Choose two pictures of chicks. Talk about all the changes you can see as the chick grows up.

The hen sits on the eggs in the nest to keep them warm.

After three weeks, the egg hatches.

The chick makes cracks in the shell.

It makes the cracks get bigger until it can get out.

Soon the chicks are dry and fluffy.

The mother hen still keeps them warm in the nest.

How do how other animals change as they grow into adults? Think about frogs, snails and butterflies. Use books and posters to find out.

adult grow

Animals and plants are living things.

Animals use their senses. They can smell, see, hear, taste or touch things.

A hawk can see a mouse.

Butterflies feed on nectar.

The mother sheep knows her lamb by smelling it.

A spider spins a web to catch flies.

A rabbit listens for danger.

Talk about each animal. How do you know it is an animal?

Most plants grow in the soil and have green leaves. Many plants have flowers and seeds.

Tall trees grow in the wood.

Ivy grows over a log.

Dandelion seeds blow away in the wind

Green grass grows in the meadow.

Daisies grow among the grass.

How do you know these are plants?

leaves **living things** **senses**

All these are animals. They look very different but they are alike in some ways.

owl

snake

zebra

crocodile

Work with a friend. Choose two of the animals on these pages. Think of ways that they are like each other.

Humans and other animals

Humans are animals too. They are like other animals in some ways.

butterfly

elephant

human

monkey

Talk about the ways humans are like each other, such as we walk on two legs and we don't have fur. What other ways can you find?

human

Humans are alike in some ways and different in others.

This is Sam.

short hair

fair hair

blue eyes

tall

thin

Are you like Sam? How are you the same? How are you different?

Here are two pictures of Viv. She looks different in the pictures but her friends all know who she is because there are some things she cannot change.

Still the same

eye colour

hair colour

face shape

height

Can you change the way you look? What stays the same? Plan some disguises. What will you change so that people do not know who you are?

All plants are alike in some ways but different in others.

These plants grow in gardens.

These wild flowers grow in fields and hedges.

Look for plants with flowers and leaves that grow near you. Draw one. Look up its name in a book.

Plants have many different parts. Some parts grow under the soil. Remember to ask before you dig up a plant.

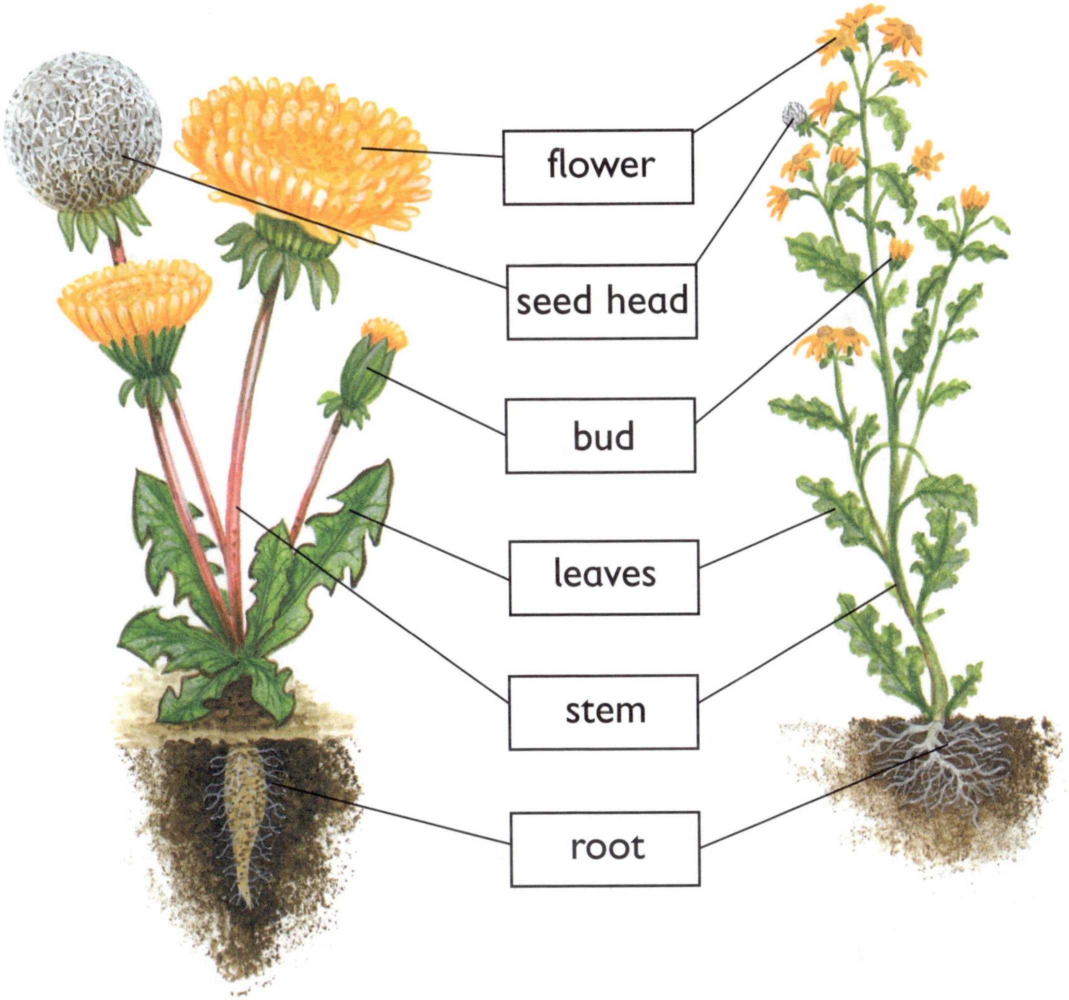

Dandelion

Groundsel

Look at these two plants. What is the same about them? What is different? Make two lists like this.

same	different

bud flower leaves root seed head stem

Trees and bushes are plants too.

You can recognise trees by the shape of their leaves. Trees often have flowers that are green or white.

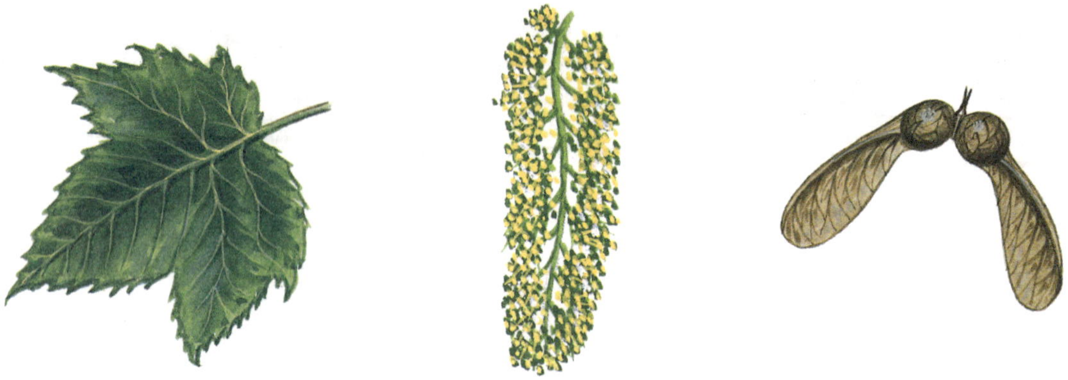

Sycamore

Holly

Look at some trees growing near your school or where you live. Find out their names.

Trees have woody trunks and branches. All trees and bushes have roots under the ground to hold them in the soil.

This is a horse chestnut tree.

Look at other trees and bushes. Can you find and describe these parts?

branch bush flower leaves root tree trunk

We are all the same in some ways and different in others. We can measure some of the differences.

James is taller than Clare.

Jamila has bigger feet than Tom.

Choose a friend. Who is taller? Who has bigger feet? Measure yourselves if you can.

Look at the size of your hands. Are they bigger than your friend's hands? How can you tell? Think of some different ways to measure hand size.

This is one way to compare your hand spans.

Measuring strip

Another way to measure your hand span is to use this measuring strip.

Will people with the biggest hand span have the biggest feet? How could you find out?

hand span

We can sort animals in different ways.

Tom has been asked to find lots of different animals near his school. These two pages show what he found.

Sort Tom's animals into 'has legs' and 'no legs'. How many are there in each group? Make a block graph to show what you find out.

There are lots of other ways to sort the animals and show the results.

Sort them by the way they move. Do they fly, walk, slither or swim? Make a pictogram and write about it. You could use a computer to sort them in another way.

pictogram **slither**

Useful science words

adult A fully grown or grown up animal.

baby A very young child or animal.

branch The woody part of a tree which grows from the trunk.

bud The part of a plant that opens into a flower.

bush A big woody plant that is smaller than a tree and without a single trunk.

child A young human.

Christmas A Christian festival.

Divali A Hindu festival.

drink To take in liquids in the way that animals do. Plants take in water but they do not drink.

exercise Energetic activity, like running or skipping.

fair test A test where most things are kept the same and only one thing is changed.

food All living things need food to stay alive.

flower The part of the plant from which the fruit and seeds grow.

Useful science words

fruit	The part of a plant where the seeds grow. We can eat some fruits like apples but some, like yew berries, are poisonous.
grow	To get bigger. All plants and animals grow.
hand span	The distance between the tip of the little finger and thumb of an outstretched hand.
human	An animal like you.
leaves	The green part of trees, bushes and other plants. We can look at the shape of the leaf to help us to find the name of a plant.
living things	Things that are alive and can grow and reproduce for example plants and animals.
medicines	Tablets, creams and liquids that people take or use when they are ill to make them better.
parent	An animal with young.
pictogram	Pictures made into a chart.
pills	One kind of medicine that people take when they are ill.
reproduce	To have young.

Useful science words

root The part of the plant that is usually underground. Roots take in water and hold it in the ground.

seeds The seed is the part of a plant that can grow into a new plant. They can start to grow with just water but need to be planted in soil to grow into healthy plants.

seed head The part of some plants that holds the seeds.

slither To move smoothly like a snail or snake.

senses There are five senses: sight, hearing, touch, taste and smell. Animals have senses that help them to find out about the world around them.

stem The stalk of a plant. The part that holds the plant up.

tally A way of counting in fives used when you want to find out how many animals or plants live in a place.

toddler A young child who is just learning to walk.

tree A big woody plant. It has roots, a woody trunk and branches, green leaves, flowers and seeds.

trunk The thick woody part of a tree that holds it up.